FRANCIS FRITH'S

ILFRACOMBE

PHOTOGRAPHIC MEMORIES

MARTIN DUNNING spent several years teaching before escaping the classroom to pursue a career as a freelance writer. He has written for the *Western Morning News* and the climbing magazine *High*, and is the author of several walking, travel and local history books. Martin has lived in Devon for 40 years, and regularly visits Ilfracombe to catch the Lundy boat.

FRANCIS FRITH'S
PHOTOGRAPHIC MEMORIES

ILFRACOMBE

PHOTOGRAPHIC MEMORIES

MARTIN DUNNING

First published in the United Kingdom in 2004 by
Frith Book Company Ltd

Limited Hardback Subscribers Edition Published in 2004
ISBN 1-85937-831-5

Paperback Edition 2004
ISBN 1-85937-832-3

British Library Cataloguing in Publication Data

Francis Frith's Ilfracombe - Photographic Memories
Martin Dunning

Frith Book Company Ltd
Frith's Barn, Teffont,
Salisbury, Wiltshire SP3 5QP
Tel: +44 (0) 1722 716 376
Email: info@francisfrith.co.uk
www.francisfrith.co.uk

Printed and bound in Great Britain

Front Cover: **ILFRACOMBE,** *The Harbour c1955* 15085
Frontispiece: **WATERMOUTH,** *Castle and Hangman
Hills c1965* W39153

*The colour-tinting is for illustrative purposes only, and is not intended
to be historically accurate*

Images 15701-15706 supplied by Martin Dunning.

CONTENTS

FRANCIS FRITH: VICTORIAN PIONEER   7

ILFRACOMBE : AN INTRODUCTION   10

ILFRACOMBE : THE HARBOUR   14

ILFRACOMBE : LANTERN HILL AND CAPSTONE HILL   28

ILFRACOMBE : THE PROMENADE   42

ILFRACOMBE : THE EDGE OF THE TOWN   56

HELE AND LEE   60

MORTHOE   65

COMBE MARTIN   69

BERRYNARBOUR   78

WATERMOUTH   82

INDEX   87

NAMES OF SUBSCRIBERS   88

Free Mounted Print Voucher   91

FRANCIS FRITH
VICTORIAN PIONEER

FRANCIS FRITH, founder of the world-famous photographic archive, was a complex and multi-talented man. A devout Quaker and a highly successful Victorian businessman, he was philosophical by nature and pioneering in outlook.

By 1855 he had already established a wholesale grocery business in Liverpool, and sold it for the astonishing sum of £200,000, which is the equivalent today of over £15,000,000. Now a very rich man, he was able to indulge his passion for travel. As a child he had pored over travel books written by early explorers, and his fancy and imagination had been stirred by family holidays to the sublime mountain regions of Wales and Scotland. 'What lands of spirit-stirring and enriching scenes and places!' he had written. He was to return to these scenes of grandeur in later years to 'recapture the thousands of vivid and tender memories', but with a different purpose. Now in his thirties, and captivated by the new science of photography, Frith set out on a series of pioneering journeys up the Nile and to the Near East that occupied him from 1856 until 1860.

INTRIGUE AND EXPLORATION

These far-flung journeys were packed with intrigue and adventure. In his life story, written when he was sixty-three, Frith tells of being held captive by bandits, and of fighting 'an awful midnight battle to the very point of surrender with a deadly pack of hungry, wild dogs'. Wearing flowing Arab costume, Frith arrived at Akaba by camel sixty years before Lawrence of Arabia, where he encountered 'desert princes and rival sheikhs, blazing with jewel-hilted swords'.

He was the first photographer to venture beyond the sixth cataract of the Nile. Africa was still the mysterious 'Dark Continent', and Stanley and Livingstone's historic meeting was a decade into the future. The conditions for picture taking confound belief. He laboured for hours in his wicker dark-room in the sweltering heat of the desert, while the volatile chemicals fizzed dangerously in their trays. Back in London he exhibited his photographs and was 'rapturously cheered' by members of the Royal Society. His reputation as a photographer was made overnight.

VENTURE OF A LIFE-TIME

Characteristically, Frith quickly spotted the opportunity to create a new business as a specialist publisher of photographs. He lived in an era of immense and sometimes violent change.

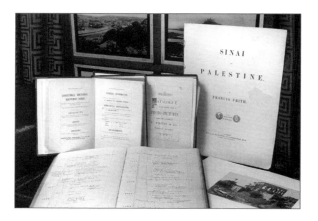

For the poor in the early part of Victoria's reign work was exhausting and the hours long, and people had precious little free time to enjoy themselves. Most had no transport other than a cart or gig at their disposal, and rarely travelled far beyond the boundaries of their own town or village. However, by the 1870s the railways had threaded their way across the country, and Bank Holidays and half-day Saturdays had been made obligatory by Act of Parliament. All of a sudden the working man and his family were able to enjoy days out and see a little of the world.

With typical business acumen, Francis Frith foresaw that these new tourists would enjoy having souvenirs to commemorate their days out. In 1860 he married Mary Ann Rosling and set out on a new career: his aim was to photograph every city, town and village in Britain. For the next thirty years he travelled the country by train and by pony and trap, producing fine photographs of seaside resorts and beauty spots that were keenly bought by millions of Victorians. These prints were painstakingly pasted into family albums and pored over during the dark nights of winter, rekindling precious memories of summer excursions.

THE RISE OF FRITH & CO

Frith's studio was soon supplying retail shops all over the country. To meet the demand he gathered about him a small team of photographers, and published the work of independent artist-photographers of the calibre of Roger Fenton and Francis Bedford. In order to gain some understanding of the scale of Frith's business one only has to look at the catalogue issued by Frith & Co in 1886: it runs to some 670 pages, listing not only many thousands of views of the British Isles but also many photographs of most European countries, and China, Japan, the USA and Canada - note the sample page shown on page 9 from the hand-written Frith & Co ledgers recording the pictures. By 1890 Frith had created the greatest specialist photographic publishing company in the world, with over 2,000 sales outlets - more than the combined number that Boots and WH Smith have today! The picture on the next page shows the Frith & Co display board at Ingleton in the Yorkshire Dales (left of window). Beautifully constructed with a mahogany frame and gilt inserts, it could display up to a dozen local scenes.

POSTCARD BONANZA

The ever-popular holiday postcard we know today took many years to develop. In 1870 the Post Office issued the first plain cards, with a pre-printed stamp on one face. In 1894 they allowed other publishers' cards to be sent through the mail with an attached adhesive halfpenny stamp. Demand grew rapidly, and in 1895 a new size of postcard was permitted called the court card, but there was little room for illustration. In 1899, a year after Frith's death, a new card measuring 5.5 x 3.5 inches became the standard format, but it was not until 1902 that the divided back came into being, so that the address and message could be on one face and a full-size illustration on the other. Frith & Co were in the vanguard of postcard development: Frith's sons Eustace and Cyril continued their father's monumental task, expanding the number of views offered to the public and recording more and more places in Britain, as the

5	·				
6	·	St Catherine's College	+	+	
7	·	Senate House & Library	+		
8	·			+	
9	·	Gerrard Hostel Bridge	+	+	+ +
3 0	·	Geological Museum		+	
1	·	Addenbrookes Hospital	+		
2	·	St Mary's Church	+		
3	·	Fitzwilliam Museum, Pitt Press &c	+		
4	·		+		
5	Buxton, The Crescent			+	
6	·	The Colonnade		+	
7	·	Public Gardens		+	
8	·			+	
9	Haddon Hall, View from the Terrace			+	
4 0	Millers Dale			+	

coasts and countryside were opened up to mass travel.

Francis Frith had died in 1898 at his villa in Cannes, his great project still growing. The archive he created continued in business for another seventy years. By 1970 it contained over a third of a million pictures showing 7,000 British towns and villages.

FRANCIS FRITH'S LEGACY

Frith's legacy to us today is of immense significance and value, for the magnificent archive of evocative photographs he created provides a unique record of change in the cities, towns and villages throughout Britain over a century and more. Frith and his fellow studio photographers revisited locations many times down the years to update their views, compiling for us an enthralling and colourful pageant of British life and character.

We are fortunate that Frith was dedicated to recording the minutiae of everyday life. For it is this sheer wealth of visual data, the painstaking chronicle of changes in dress, transport, street layouts, buildings, housing, engineering and landscape that captivates us so much today. His remarkable images offer us a powerful link with the past and with the lives of our ancestors.

THE VALUE OF THE ARCHIVE TODAY

Computers have now made it possible for Frith's many thousands of images to be accessed almost instantly. Frith's images are increasingly used as visual resources, by social historians, by researchers into genealogy and ancestry, by architects and town planners, and by teachers involved in local history projects.

In addition, the archive offers every one of us an opportunity to examine the places where we and our families have lived and worked down the years. Highly successful in Frith's own era, the archive is now, a century and more on, entering a new phase of popularity. Historians consider the Francis Frith Collection to be of prime national importance. It is the only archive of its kind remaining in private ownership. Francis Frith's archive is now housed in an historic timber barn in the beautiful village of Teffont in Wiltshire. Its founder would not recognize the archive office as it is today. In place of the many thousands of dusty boxes containing glass plate negatives and an all-pervading odour of photographic chemicals, there are now ranks of computer screens. He would be amazed to watch his images travelling round the world at unimaginable speeds through internet lines.

The archive's future is both bright and exciting. Francis Frith, with his unshakeable belief in making photographs available to the greatest number of people, would undoubtedly approve of what is being done today with his lifetime's work. His photographs depicting our shared past are now bringing pleasure and enlightenment to millions around the world a century and more after his death.

ILFRACOMBE
AN INTRODUCTION

ILFRACOMBE is recorded in the *Domesday Book* as Alfreincoma, a Saxon name which roughly translates as 'the combe of the sons of Alfred', but long before Alfred and his family settled in the valley the surrounding hills had been occupied. Hillsborough, rising 500 feet above the sea and accessible only from the south, was the site of an Iron Age fort built by the Dumnonii tribe in around 300BC, and a Bronze Age cist discovered here in the 1930s suggests that the site may have been settled even earlier.

Hillsborough had the advantage of being easily defended, but it has no natural water supply, and the steep, exposed slopes would hardly have made for comfortable living; moreover, at the foot of Hillsborough lay a sheltered cove. The North Devon coast is exposed to the might of the Atlantic and swept by powerful tides, and in the lee of Lantern Hill – probably then an island at high tide – ships could find a safe haven, practically the only one east of the estuary of the Taw and the Torridge.

The deep valleys were ideal for the raising of vegetables, and inland lay good grazing. With travel over land being something of a trial thanks to the mud and the hills, the majority of trade took place by boat, and soon Ilfracombe became a flourishing port. Success in trade, however, brought with it other, less benign demands. Successive kings, prosecuting this war or that, cast greedy eyes on the growing fleet: in 1208 King John collected men and ships to fight in Ireland, in 1302 Edward I demanded from Ilfracombe ships for the war against Scotland, and in 1346 the town provided Edward III with six ships and 82 men for the siege of Calais.

There were other distractions from the pursuit of commerce. Duties levied on the silver mined at nearby Combe Martin, and taxes on salt and wool and later alcohol, all contributed to the development of a small but healthy smuggling industry. And where there are ships and trade, there almost inevitably follows the odd bit of piracy. Lundy, 25 miles to the east and in the middle of the Bristol Channel trade routes, was frequently used as a pirate stronghold, notably by the Marisco family, while in the 16th century Ilfracombe was subject to raids by Irish pirates.

Trade flourished, however, despite piracy, storms and the occasional intrusion of greater affairs such as the Civil War, during which Ilfracombe held out for Parliament before falling in 1644 to Sir Francis Dodington. By the reign of Charles II, Ilfracombe vessels were trading regularly with Llanelli, Swansea and Tenby. In 1678 the quay is recorded as being 216ft long, and its cobbles would have been piled high with all manner of cargo. Harbour records for 1686, for example, record the *Happy Returns* of Ilfracombe landing 'five tanned hides, two tonns of Iron and Iron Wares, one box of Haberdashery Wares … Three groce of Corkes, one cask of salt, Six hundred wt of soape, one hundred wt of Brass & Pewter, one baskitt of earthen wares, two baskits of port and Spanish Wines.'

In 1771 there was a report in the *Exeter Flying Post* of six women arriving in Ilfracombe 'for the benefit of the air, salt water and to spend part of the summer season', and in 1794 the *Universal British Directory* described the town as 'a pleasant and convenient place for bathing'. The tourist industry, which was to become the lifeblood of the town, had begun.

Business, even as early as 1823, was brisk enough to justify the engagement of Welsh miners to cut the tunnels which opened up more beaches for bathers, but the tourists of the early 19th century must have been of hardier stock than today's visitors: the coach from Bath took twenty-four bone-shaking hours to reach Ilfracombe.

Despite the influx of tourists, Ilfracombe had not changed enormously: a tithe map of 1840 shows an almost medieval, linear town running from the church at the top down to the harbour. The sanitary arrangements were pretty medieval, too, and in 1849 there was a serious outbreak of cholera. A Board of Health Inspector's report the following year was so damning that the council were forced into action; they formed their own Board of Health, which instituted the building of a sewage works in 1851 and a reservoir in 1866.

Alongside the tourist trade, the old industries carried on. Fishermen landed huge catches of herrings and pilchards, and when the fishing

ILFRACOMBE, *The View from the Gilbert Curate Hotel 1911* 63898

was poor they could always supplement their income by taking the more adventurous visitors out to, say, Hele Bay. Shipbuilding carried on until the latter part of the 19th century, with the *Duchess of Clarence*, launched in 1828, being the largest home-built vessel at 274 tons. The trading ketches, too, were busy. For centuries they had brought Welsh limestone for the limekilns, but increasingly they carried building materials: the yellow bricks that are such a feature of Ilfracombe's Victorian villas and hotels, and limestone not for burning but to construct the stout walls of the harbour and the pier.

Advancement (with a capital A) was the great Victorian watchword, and the entrepreneurs of Ilfracombe were no more immune to the heady whiff of progress than their counterparts in more cosmopolitan places. The true measure of a town's ambitions lay in its ability to attract the ultimate symbol of success – the railway. The investment required to bring the railway to an out-of-the-way spot like Ilfracombe needed a certain vision, and the town's businessmen had that in spades. The stated intention of the

founders of the Ilfracombe Joint Stock Land and Investment Company was to make Ilfracombe the 'Brighton of the West'; to modern ears, this has a touch of the folie de grandeur about it, but the efforts of these men and those of the Ilfracombe Hotel and Esplanade Company, along with plenty of others more anonymous, made the dreams a reality.

The vast, neo-Gothic edifice of the Ilfracombe Hotel, a hugely ambitious project, opened in 1867. The railway arrived in 1874, the year after Sir Bourchier Palk Wrey's building of the Promenade Pier, and the stage was set for what many regard as Ilfracombe's golden age.

Nothing typifies Ilfracombe's success more than the paddle steamers. Before the building of the pier the paddlers had been regular visitors, but docking was difficult, and often they would anchor with the passengers having to be ferried off by rowing boat. Now the steamers could tie up alongside the pier, and disembarking passengers was merely a matter of pushing up the gangplank. The ship-owning Campbell family moved from the Clyde to Bristol in 1880 to take

ILFRACOMBE *1923* 74948

advantage of the potential of the Bristol Channel trade, and their white-funnelled vessels soon became a common sight; the first Campbell paddle steamer, the *Waverley*, arrived in Ilfracombe in 1887. As industry around the shores of the Bristol Channel boomed, so did the paddle steamers. Trips were run to Ilfracombe from Swansea, Barry and Cardiff, carrying day-tripping miners and steel workers, and the sheer volume of passengers disembarked is mind-boggling. On the August Bank Holiday of 1905 the *Britannia*, the *Westward Ho!*, the *Albion*, the *Brighton*, the *Normandy*, the *Ravenswood* and the *Gwalia* all visited, carrying 400 to 800 passengers each to a resort which at the time had a population of around 8,000. In 1906, a total of 164,745 passengers disembarked.

The hoteliers, publicans, sellers of cream teas and souvenir shop owners were no doubt delighted, but there was the odd dissenting voice. The paddle steamers were not licensed to sell alcohol, and their stays were limited by the enormous tides of the Bristol Channel, so that that their passengers – understandably, as this was a rare chance to let their hair down – consumed beer at such a rate that in 1896 questions were asked in the Houses of Parliament about Ilfracombe's problems with drunken Welsh folk.

Despite the bustle of the tourist trade, not all was well; by the mid 1920s the Ilfracombe Hotel had recorded its first loss, a circumstance which led to the west wing being let out for office space - this marked the beginning of the hotel's decline. The paddlers were still profitable, however – some had been lost in World War I when they were converted for use as minesweepers, but most returned to the Bristol Channel, and as late as 1946 the business was considered healthy enough for the Campbells to launch a new ship. The magnificent *Bristol Queen*, capable of carrying 600 passengers, arrived in Ilfracombe for the first time on 14 September, greeted by the firing of rockets. This was the last fling of a dying trade, however; over the years the paddler fleet slipped away, and today only one remains afloat – the *Waverley*, which visits for a couple of weeks each summer.

The latter half of the 20th century could be seen as a period of decline for Ilfracombe: the railway fell to the Beeching axe in 1974, and two years later, after a long rearguard action by local campaigners, the Ilfracombe Hotel was demolished. Sir Bourchier Palk Wrey's promenade pier just made it into the 21st century, but now that, too, has gone.

On summer days, though, the town will still be crowded with visitors, who might take in a show at the Landmark Theatre, built on the site of the Ilfracombe Hotel. The striking Victorian hotels, villas and terraces remain, and two or three times a week the MS *Oldenburg* docks to take on 250 passengers bound for Lundy. The harbour bustles, the pubs, cafes and fish and chips shops do a brisk trade, and the seagulls fight over pasty crusts. And from the heights of Hillsborough, looking down over the harbour, this handsome little Victorian town looks much the same as when Francis Frith's photographer first visited in the 1870s.

ILFRACOMBE: THE HARBOUR

RAPPAREE COVE *c1875* 5243

The cove was originally called Raperee Cove; it got its name at the time of the 1598 Irish uprising, when Ilfracombe was raided by Irish pirates who took their name from the pike-like weapon they carried - the raperee.

15

THE HARBOUR
c1875 7967

At the top of Lantern Hill (centre right), 100 feet above sea level, stands the Chapel of St Nicholas, patron saint of sailors, fittingly enough, and also of scholars. Probably the oldest building in the town, built in the early 14th century, the chapel has also functioned as a laundry, a home for a family of sixteen, and a lighthouse.

► **FROM ABOVE RAPPAREE COVE**
c1875 5241

Sir Bourchier Palk Wrey, Lord of the Manor, had to obtain a £10,000 loan and a special Act of Parliament for the building of the Promenade Pier, which was opened on 15 May 1873.

◄ **THE ENTRANCE TO THE HARBOUR**
c1875 5248

Standing guard over the entrance to the harbour is the 447ft eminence of Hillsborough, easily defended and probably the first settlement in the area. A Bronze Age cist was unearthed here in the 1930s, and there is a major earthwork fort at the summit, which is thought to have been built by the Dumnonii in 300BC.

▲ **THE PIER ENTRANCE** *2004* I5701

The road here was originally much narrower (see 5241, p.18), but in 1893-95 the pier was widened, involving the demolition of the Golden Lion, a popular harbourside pub, which stood on the left. Now the open area of the pier (empty in 5241) is a busy car park.

◄**THE PIER** *2003* I5702

The round promenade pier - the last of its type - was demolished, to howls of protest, in 2001. One link with the past remains, however, in the shape of the *Waverley*, the last sea-going paddle steamer in the world, which still visits each summer. At 240ft long, she is just 10ft short of the size limit for the harbour.

▼ **FROM RAPPAREE** *1894* 33436

The bathing huts here were nearly the scene of a diplomatic incident in 1878. Alfred Price, son of the huts' owner, tried to stop a young man throwing stones at the huts, and a fight broke out. The young man turned out to be none other than Prince Frederick Wilhelm - later Kaiser Wilhelm II. The incident was hushed up, but in World War I Alfred Price became a local hero.

► **FROM CORONATION TERRACE** *1891* 22911

Several generations of the Bourchier family were responsible for the growth of the harbour, building and enlarging the inner wall from 1766 onwards. In 1823 a storm severely damaged the inner wall, causing the Bourchiers to dig into their pockets yet again.

◄ **THE *VELINDRA*
APPROACHING
THE PIER**
1890 22914

The *Velindra* was just
one of the paddle
steamers that were the
lifeblood of
Ilfracombe's tourist
industry in the latter
part of the 19th
century and the first
half of the 20th. Before
the building of the
pier, passengers often
had to be ferried to
and from the
steamers, which
anchored off Warp
House Point.

► **THE HARBOUR**
1911 63912

The two-masted vessel
in the centre of the
harbour is typical of
the many ketches that
worked the coast -
sturdy, no-nonsense
boats which carried
everything from
cooking pots to coal.
One of the most
famous was the *Kate*,
which worked from
Ilfracombe for 40 years.

FROM HILLSBOROUGH
1911 63892

The lifeboat station, on the pier just south of Lantern Hill, was built in the 1860s at a cost of £222 15s, replacing the lifeboat station at Hiern's Lane. The building of the Promenade pier meant that the lifeboat had to be towed round the harbour to Broad Street for launching.

THE HARBOUR *2004* I5703

Beyond the slipway (centre) are the open doors of the new lifeboat station, built in 1984 and housing the *Spirit of Derbyshire*, a Mersey Class boat capable of 16 knots and with a range of 145 nautical miles. The old lifeboat station on the pier now houses the Aquarium.

HILLSBOROUGH FROM THE HARBOUR *c1935* I5006

The boat here is probably the *Snowflake*, a 66ft Clyde 'puffer' of 73 tons built in 1895; she was operated from 1897-1941 by the Irwin family, carrying coal from South Wales in the winter and strawberries in the summer. How many cream teas in a full cargo?

23

THE HARBOUR FROM ST JAMES' GARDENS
c1935 I5042

It is a quiet day for the paddle steamers, with a mere two moored at the pier. In their heyday there might be as many as six moored abreast to the pier, and passengers had to disembark by hopping from one ship to the next.

ST JAMES' GARDENS *c1935* I5026

During World War I, several of the paddlers were converted for use as minesweepers. The *Brighton Queen* hit a mine off Ostend in 1915 and sank, a fate which also befell the *Lady Ismay*. The *Barry* managed to survive the carnage of the Dardanelles, and returned to tourist duty in 1919.

THE HARBOUR *c1955* I5086

The Royal Britannia Hotel (centre left) was built in the 18th century, and was then named merely the Britannia. In October 1856, however, the future Edward VII, then aged fifteen, stayed at the hotel, which soon after adopted the 'Royal' prefix.

25

THE HARBOUR *c1955* I5130

On the far right, opposite the end of the pier and hidden by the
Devon mist, is Larkstone Cove, site of a lime kiln where Welsh
coal burnt Welsh limestone to produce the lime that was vital to
regulate the acidity of the local soil. The cove was also used for
loading and discharging ballast.

FORE STREET *c1935* I5005

At the bottom of Fore Street - down by the harbour and therefore handy for the maritime fraternity - are two pubs, the George and the Prince of Wales, both of which claim to be the oldest hostelry in town.

LANTERN HILL
c1875 5245

Despite the lofty heights surrounding Ilfracombe, the town centre is low-lying and prone to flooding. In 1910 the sea breached the sturdy sea wall above Cheyne Beach (centre) and caused a surge which flooded Ropery Meadow and damaged roads. Although often referred to as a storm, one school of thought maintains that this was in fact a tsunami caused by an earthquake in the Bristol Channel.

FROM THE TORS
c1870 5238

During Victoria's reign, Ilfracombe changed from being a largely linear settlement, stretching along the valley, and spread itself up the surrounding hills. The three most important elements of Victorian growth can be seen here: the terraces on the right, the swanky villas of Tors Park in the foreground, and the Ilfracombe Hotel (centre left) with its improbably large flag.

ILFRACOMBE: LANTERN HILL AND CAPSTONE HILL

► **FROM CAPSTONE PARADE** *c1875* 5244

Wildersmouth Beach - named after Wilder Brook - was the main beach before the cutting of the tunnels. Here, one morning in 1817, the Georgian novelist Fanny Burney wandered out onto the beach and became cut off by the tide. Capstone Parade had yet to be cut, and she was forced to wait until dusk to return.

◄ **FROM CAPSTONE HILL**
c1875 5242

The Ilfracombe Hotel (centre left) was built by the Ilfracombe Hotel and Esplanade Company. The imposing yellow brick Gothic Revival building, with 210 rooms and a 1,000ft terrace, put Ilfracombe in the first rank of resorts when it was opened on 15 May 1867. At 9am daily a coach left to meet the train at Barnstaple, returning at 5.30pm.

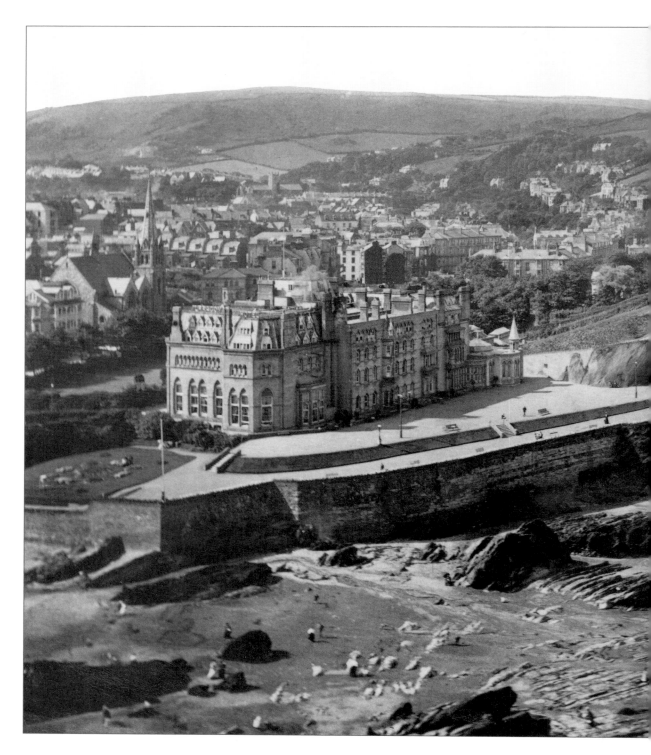

FROM CAPSTONE HILL *1906* 56786

In 1925 the Ilfracombe Hotel recorded its first trading loss of £245. In 1928 the west wing was rented to the council for use as offices, but the rot had set in. Decades of genteel decline followed, and in 1976 the hotel was demolished, despite a 16,000-signature petition and a letter from Sir John Betjeman bemoaning its loss.

THE LANDMARK THEATRE *2004* I5704

The 483-seat theatre was built on the old Ilfracombe Hotel site, and was opened by the actor Joss Ackland in 1998. The two cones, built of white Belgian brick as an echo of the pale bricks of the old hotel, have over 300,000 bricks between them.

▶ **HILLSBOROUGH AND LANTERN HILL** *1923* 74932

Although steam was dominant by the twenties (a paddle steamer can just be seen approaching the harbour), sail still hung on stubbornly - on the far right, just above the roofs of the harbourside, we can see the masts of sailing schooners.

◀ **AT SUNSET** *1911* 63911

The Granville Hotel, looking like something out of a Scooby Doo adventure here, was built on a spectacular site - perhaps the best in town - in 1891. It was a temperance hotel, named after the leading 19th-century temperance activist Dr Granville, and designed as a mock castle by W H Gould.

▲ **LANTERN HILL** *1899* 43112

Lantern Hill and the Chapel of St Nicholas are not just a focal point for visitors; for centuries the light on the chapel was a vital navigational aid for mariners. It was considered so important that as early as the 16th century Bishop Veysey granted indulgences to anyone who contributed to the upkeep of the light.

◀ **FROM CAPSTONE HILL** *c1870* 5240

On the left, just below the skyline, is Hillsborough Terrace, and in front of it is Sir Bourchier Palk Wrey's house, now the Cliff Hydro Hotel. Coronation Terrace (centre) was started to celebrate the coronation of George IV in 1821, but it was not completed until 1828.

FROM CAPSTONE HILL *1899* 43107

The flat-roofed properties along the Promenade were built by the ubiquitous W H Gould in 1880. In the foreground on the beach is a Punch and Judy show, an evergreen attraction which here appears in danger of being swept away by the boisterous Bristol Channel swell.

CAPSTONE PARADE *c1935* I5039

The cutting of Capstone Parade was undertaken in 1843 to provide work for the unemployed men of the town. The cost was £220 - something of a bargain when you consider just how much rock had to be shifted. At the opening there were fireworks, a public tea, and two balls - one for the workers and one for the gentry, who were unwilling, one assumes, to mix with the great unwashed!

THE BEACH *1923* 74951

Capstone Parade was designed to be 'suitable for bath chairs', as
can be seen by its level passage around Capstone Hill. It would be
nice to think of this as an early example of disability awareness,
but the truth is more prosaic: a level promenade was more likely
to attract the infirm and elderly and their carers, thus boosting
the profits of Ilfracombe's hoteliers.

COLLINGWOOD AND THE SHELTER
1894 33451

The Wesleyan chapel (centre left) was built in 1864 to replace the original chapel of 1830. When this picture was taken, the chapel was not long for this world: it was due to be demolished in 1895, as the council wanted to open up the area to create the promenade.

CAPSTONE HILL FROM THE WEST
c1875 5250

This shows the northern slope of Capstone Hill and its junction with Ropery Meadow (centre, in front of the chapel) as it was before any development took place. Within a few years, the area by the little curving lane would be dominated by the Victoria Pavilion. In the foreground, the area later occupied by the Granville Hotel is still being farmed.

ILFRACOMBE: THE PROMENADE

▼ **THE PROMENADE** *2004* I5705

This photograph was taken from Batten's Corner, just to the left of the Wesleyan chapel in picture 33451 (p.42). The slim spire in the distance is that of Emmanuel Church, the Wesleyan chapel's replacement, built in 1898 on a narrow plot given by the council.

▶ **ST PHILIP'S CHURCH** *1890* 22940

'The Church of Pip and Jim', as it is locally known, was the first Gothic Revival building in the town, designed by John Hayward in 1856. Hayward was Devon's most prolific church designer of the 19th century, with at least 28 churches built from scratch and several restorations.

◄ THE VICTORIA PAVILION
1894 33452

The Victoria Pavilion, 200 feet long and 35 feet wide, was built at a cost of £4,000 for the Queen's Golden Jubilee in 1888. Its glass and wrought iron design by W H Gould was compared with Crystal Palace, although the locals called it the Cucumber Frame.

► THE VICTORIA PAVILION
The Interior 1894 33453

Behind the two pillars (centre left) is the stage, venue in the 1920s for Saturday evening concerts by the 12-piece Ilfracombe Orchestra led by Guy Magrath. Another attraction was the town band, resplendent in their polished buttons and peaked caps, who played three times daily here or in the bandstand.

CAPSTONE HILL
1906 56785

The zigzag paths on what was once known as Capstan Hill were cut in 1894. The hillside to the right was often used to celebrate events, with local people forming up to spell out words such as Empire Day (24 May 1909) and Peace, the latter on 19 July 1919, the day on which World War One was officially recognised as over.

47

THE PROMENADE
1911 63900A

This flat, open area -
Ropery Meadow - was
for many years used to
make ropes, using hemp
from Combe Martin. In
1872 it was bought by
the council for £2,203.
On Victoria Pavilion
there are now the initials
GR, honouring King
George V who came to
the throne in 1910.

THE PROMENADE *1923* 74943

The Promenade was modernised in 1922; gone are the paths, to be replaced by a putting green. Another absentee is the fountain (visible in 63900A, centre). This had been donated in 1890 by Edward Joseph, but it was removed in 1922 and sold for £12.

THE PARADE AND THE BANDSTAND *1923* 74949

The bandstand, built in 1894 and demolished in 1970, was open only on its east side. The west side was glassed in to prevent the prevailing westerlies removing the bandsmen's sheet music and caps. The bandstand recently reappeared, fully restored, in Wolverhampton.

► **CAPSTONE HILL**
1926 79219

The 750-seat Victoria Pavilion Theatre was opened on 18 May 1925. The cost was £8,000, compared with £4,000 for the original pavilion; twice the price, but something of a bargain when you consider that 40 years had passed. Inflation was obviously slower in those days.

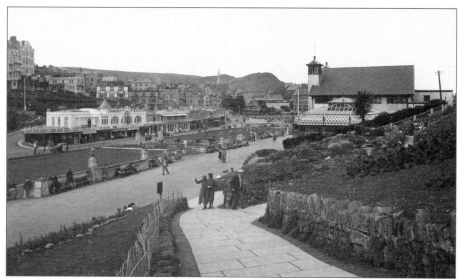

◄ **VICTORIA PROMENADE**
c1935 15030

On the left, sporting its distinctive turret, is the Gaiety Concert Hall, built in 1910 and here playing host to the Concord Follies. It is flanked on either side by Funland and Sportland - reminders that despite fifties austerity, people were determined to have a good time.

▲ THE VIEW FROM CAPSTONE HILL *c1960* I5176

The Collingwood Hotel (left, above the roof of the theatre) is also visible in photographs 5240 (p.37) and 33451 (p.42), showing clearly its transformation from a rather plain terrace to the balconied extravagance of later years. The Collingwood was where W H Gould spent his final years, as proprietor.

◄ FEEDING THE SEA GULLS *c1955* I5126

Some things change, some things remain: the trilby and the short-back-and-sides have long been consigned to the waste basket of history, but the blizzard of gulls, squabbling over pasty crusts and chips, is still an unavoidable part of seaside life.

▼ THE LADIES' BATHING BEACH *1890* 22927

Welsh miners were employed to cut the tunnels in 1823. Bathing was strictly segregated; one observer noted that 'the westward part is allotted to Gentlemen, while the eastward is by custom left to the ladies and is carefully guarded against all intrusion', a state of affairs that lasted until 1905, when mixed bathing was permitted.

▶ THE BATH HOUSE
2004 I5706

The Bath House, with its elegant Greek portico, was built in 1836 by the Ilfracombe Sea Bathing Company, and provided hot and cold sea-water baths for its patrons. The entrance to the tunnels is round to the right of the Bath House.

◄ **THE BATHING POOL** *1911* 63907

The building on the cliff in the distance was erected as two houses in the 1890s and converted by a millionaire to a single dwelling in 1915. In the 1920s it became the Beacon Castle Hotel. It eventually burnt down in a spectacular blaze on 16 May 1985 which took 11 fire crews to extinguish. The site is now occupied by flats, built in 1988.

► **THE CARLTON HOTEL** *c1965* I5232

The Carlton was built as two villas in 1850, on a field overlooking Runnymead Meadows. As was the case with many villas, the scent of money from the tourist trade led to them being converted, first as St Petroc's Boarding House and finally as the Carlton Hotel.

▶ **THE BELGRAVE HOTEL**
1890 22938

The Belgrave was built in 1884 on Wilder Road by W M Robbins, who also designed the Royal Clarence Hotel and some villas in Torrs Park. An early advertising slogan for the Belgrave was 'Sanitary Arrangements Perfect', probably chosen to counter the memory of the cholera outbreak earlier in the century. The Belgrave is now the Berkeley Hotel.

◀ **TORS PARK FROM THE ZIGZAG**
1890 22934

In 1860, intending to make Ilfracombe the 'Brighton of the West', a group of businessmen founded the Ilfracombe Joint Stock Land and Investment Company and commenced the building of villas at Torrs Park. Several of these villas later became schools: Ilfracombe College, the Convent of the Immaculate Conception, and Hereford House School, all of which flourished around the turn of the century.

54

▲ **THE PARISH CHURCH** *1899* 43119

The first church here was a Saxon one, built from timber. The Normans followed, but the base of their tower is all that remains. The present Holy Trinity dates from the early 14th century, when the Bishop decreed, on pain of a £40 penalty, that the church should be enlarged to cater for the growing congregation.

◄**THE PARISH CHURCH AND THE GARDEN OF REMEMBRANCE** *c1935* I5009

This is a classic site for a church - on a hillock that is easy to defend. The Memorial Gardens, with a granite column topped with the bronze-winged figure of Victory, were opened by Lord Fortescue in 1924. Bronze panels commemorate the 157 men of the parish who fell in World War I; more panels were later added in memory of the 59 who died in World War II.

ILFRACOMBE: THE EDGE OF THE TOWN

THE TORRS WALK *1911* 63909

The pavilion at the top of The Torrs was a noted refreshment spot, and for 2d (adults) or 1d (children) visitors could walk to the summit at 451ft. Some may have been put off, however, by a 1900s guidebook which gave the height of the summit as 2,600ft!

▶ **FROM THE TORRS** *1899* 43109

The Torrs walk thoughtfully skirts the ridge of the Seven Hills, and it was of a sufficiently shallow gradient to allow less energetic visitors to take a pony and trap to the top. The pavilion and flagpole were taken down in 1964, and in 1967 the National Trust bought the Torrs and the Seven Hills.

◀ **SLADE VALLEY FROM THE CAIRN** *1911* 63917

After 20 years of lobbying, fund raising, and the obtaining of an Act of Parliament, the London and South West Railway arrived in Ilfracombe on 21 July 1874 (note the steam train on the left). The last train left Ilfracombe Station at 7.55pm on 3 October 1970 carrying 500 passengers, and the large railhead site eventually became a factory.

▲ **THE CAIRN FROM THE WEST** *1911* 63915

At 511ft, Cairn Top is the highest of the hills overlooking the town. In the mid 19th century the council rented the west side of the Cairn from E W Veale, a local solicitor, before buying the whole area for £910 in 1899. In 1974 the Devon Trust for Nature Conservation rented the site from the council and turned it into a nature reserve.

◄ **CHAMBERCOMBE VALLEY** *1911* 63918

Chambercombe is an ancient manor, named after the de Cambernon family, one of whom fought alongside William the Conqueror at Hastings. In 1098 Jordan de Cambernon came to Ilfracombe, and his descendants - variously known as the Champernouns, the Chambernons and the Chambrons - were lords of the manor and occasionally rectors of Holy Trinity until in the 17th century the manor was sold off.

HELE AND LEE

HELE
The Bay and Hillsborough 1923 74959

Hele is a name found commonly in Devon, and comes from the Saxon 'healh', meaning 'sheltered valley'. The east slope of Hillsborough was heavily cultivated in much the same way as the valleys of Combe Martin were (see 79239, p.77). The beach was used for landing coal from vessels such as the *Snowflake* and the *Salina Mary*, a trade which ended in the 1930s.

61

◀ **THE COAST ROAD TO LEE** *1911* 63919

R D Blackmore, author of *Lorna Doone*, was moved to describe the walk to Lee as 'one of the finest in England'. In 1856 the novelist George Eliot, visiting with her partner George Lewes, was also mightily impressed with this scenery.

◄ HELE
*From the Cliffs
1923* 74954

Lewis's Beach Tea House (far right) was renowned for its cream teas. So popular did it become that on rainy days large canvas tarpaulins would be erected outside as awnings to keep the crowds dry. There was also the Better Hole, opened after World War I, which became the Fort Cafe in 1937.

▲ **LEE,** *From the Golf Links 1911* 63923

Lee was a favoured spot for smugglers, who did not do things by halves - in September 1820 it is recorded that 1,500 gallons of brandy and gin were landed here in one night. Alcohol was not the only profitable commodity; salt was also brought ashore to avoid the tax levied on it.

◄ LEE
The Post Office 1911
63929

On the day Queen Victoria died, the postmistress at Lee's old post office was taking down a telegram announcing the Queen's death when she was struck by lightning in the left eye and blinded. The low building at the back is the new post office, opened in 1900 but now closed.

LEE
The Post Office
c1965 L27049

Lee's distinctive herringbone walls (centre) date from the 1870s, when Robert Wilson, an early species of property developer, embarked on an extensive development of the village. John Cousins, Wilson's foreman, built the walls from local stone and planted many fuchsias, which led in time to Lee becoming known as Fuchsia Valley, and even having a song written about it.

LEE, *Old Maids Cottage c1950* L27050

This was built as a much smaller cottage in 1653, and rebuilt in the 1870s by Robert Wilson. He thatched many of the buildings, but over time most have reverted to slate roofs - this is one of the few still thatched. The name comes from a local poem which tells of three young women who were so picky about would-be husbands that they ended up as *The Three Old Maids of Lee.*

MORTEHOE

MORTEHOE, *Morte Point from Bull Point c1900* M99504

Morte Point's reputation as a sailors' graveyard was never more deserved than on 26 October 1859 when eight ships - the *I'll Try*, the *Matthew Thompson*, the *Rose*, the *Thistle*, the *Hannah*, the *Clara*, the *Anne*, and the *William Robertson*, were lost. From one ship, all the crew survived; from the other seven, all but four men were lost.

MORTEHOE, *Windy Point, Morte Point 1935* 87129

The sharp fangs of the Morte Slates have ripped through the hulls of many vessels. Locals regarded wrecks as fair game, and often the survivors were killed to prevent news of the sinking getting out. One charming woman named Elizabeth Berry was reputed to have held sailors under with a pitchfork until they drowned.

MORTEHOE
*Bull Point
Lighthouse 1890*
22967

The lighthouse was built in 1879 at a cost of £7,000. Bull Point was chosen as the site because it was more economical to build it here. The Bristol Channel pilots had wanted the lighthouse built at Morte Point itself; the wreckers did not want it at all! A landslide severely damaged the lighthouse in 1972, and while it was being repaired a lightship was anchored offshore.

MORTEHOE, *Rockham Beach c1965* M99035

Despite the presence of the lighthouse, some sinkings still occurred. In January 1914 the SS *Collier* struck the rocks, but this time there was to be a happy ending. The SS *Devonia* rescued the crew of eight, and also took aboard the Collier's dog, cat and goldfish!

MORTEHOE, *The Church 1935* 87130

The church of St Mary Magdalene stands opposite the pub, which is named the Ship Aground for obvious reasons. The chancel arch in the church sports an enormous and very striking mosaic, put up in 1905 in memory of the churchwarden's wife, and made by the craftsmen who had worked on St Paul's Cathedral.

COMBE MARTIN

COMBE MARTIN, *The Bay c1871* 5900

This photograph was taken from Small Mouth, just east of Watermouth. In the middle distance are the rocks of Outer Stone, and on the opposite side of the bay, Little Hangman rises to 716 feet. The name comes from the Saxon 'hang', or 'slope', and the Celtic 'mynedd', meaning hill - therefore the Sloping Hill, and nothing to do with the noose.

▼ **COMBE MARTIN,** *A Rest on the Way to Hangman Hill c1955* C145031

The slopes between Little Hangman and Sherrycombe, to the east, were often descended by local women to gather laver (seaweed) from The Rawns. It was carried in 20lb bundles up the steep cliffside and taken home to be cooked with vinegar and bacon. Laver is still served in local cafes today.

▶ **THE HUNTER'S INN** *c1950* I5051

The Heddon Valley is often called the 'Switzerland of England', so when the original thatched inn burned down in 1895, the owner, Colonel Lake, decided to rebuild in the style of a Swiss chalet. It has since been considerably extended and altered.

COMBE MARTIN
Woodlands and Furze Park 1935
87067

Combe Martin (or Combmartin as it was known until the 1890s) takes its name from Robert FitzMartin, the first lord of the manor, whose family retained the title until the 14th century. The village stretches along the valley of the River Umber, and is reputed to have the longest main street of any village in the country - nearly two miles.

▶ **COMBE MARTIN**
General View 1930
83463

Combe Martin's early prosperity came from its lead and silver mines, which were worked from prehistoric times. So important were the mines that in Edward I's reign 300 miners from Derby were brought down to work them. Remains still litter the valley: the odd shape in the field above and to the left of the church tower is an old mine.

▶ **COMBE MARTIN**
A Devon Lane
1937 88186

The tunnel in the right-hand wall ran into Clogg's Quarry, which supplied limestone to the eight limekilns in the valley. The south side of the valley is riddled with old quarries, including Park Quarry, Hoyle's Quarry and Harris's Quarry. Surprisingly, the lime industry was more dangerous than the mines.

◀ **COMBE MARTIN**
The Church and the War Memorial 1930
83468

The 13th-century church of St Peter ad Vincula is built of red sandstone. On its south door is a Sanctuary Ring, which enabled criminals who clasped it to be spared punishment if they confessed their wrongdoings and left the country.

▲ **COMBE MARTIN,** *The Pack of Cards Hotel 1926* 79248

Known until 1933 as the Kings Arms, the Pack of Cards was built in 1626 as a town house by George Ley to celebrate a win at cards. The building mirrors a pack of cards, with 52 windows (some of them filled in to avoid window tax) and four floors (for the four suits), each with 13 doors.

◄**COMBE MARTIN**
The Harbour 1911
63963

It is thought that the first ocean-going ships to visit this harbour belonged to the Phoenicians, who came to trade for silver around 400BC. The ketches here are of a less exotic origin - they probably crossed the Bristol Channel from South Wales with cargoes of coal and limestone.

COMBE MARTIN
The Strand 1926 79236

Harbour hotels see their share
of odd events. On 17 March
1891 six men appeared out of
a blizzard in a small boat,
having rowed several miles
after their barquentine *Ethel*
went aground at
Heddonsmouth. Apparently
none the worse for their
experience, they were
entertained by Captain John
Ley at the Marine Hotel (left).

▼ **COMBE MARTIN,** *Seaside Hill and the Harbour c1955* C145048

The lorry coming down the hill (left) is a sign of changing times; by the fifties most goods were being moved by road, and the ketches seen in photograph 63963 (p.73) were long gone. The harbour is still busy, but the cargo for the local boatmen now is a human one - holidaymakers on a sightseeing trip.

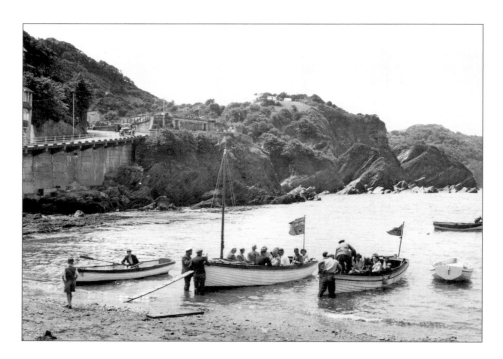

► **COMBE MARTIN**
Sandy Cove c1965
C145172

Spring bank holiday here sees the odd tradition of the Hunting of the Earl of Rone, an old pagan ritual involving a hobby horse (as at Padstow and Helston) and the chasing of the 'Earl' through the woods before he is mounted backwards on a donkey and led in procession to the beach.

COMBE MARTIN
Newbury Beach
1926 79239

The deep, sheltered valleys of this part of the coast were at one time noted for their market gardens, which grew a variety of produce, but were most famous for their strawberries. The Clyde puffer *Snowflake* (see I5006, page 23) operated from Combe Martin by the Irwin family, regularly set sail in the summer for Wales with a hold full of fruit.

► **COMBE MARTIN**
The Sterrage Valley
1911 63951

The Sterrage Valley (sometimes spelled Sterridge) was a popular spot for day trips, initially by horse and coach such as those run by Copp's, and from 1910 onwards by charabanc. Copp's coaching trips then became Copp's Silver Cars, and competition came from W H Gubb's Lucky Violet charabancs.

BERRYNARBOR
The Village
Street 1911 63947

By 1911 the
population of
Berrynarbor was
around 600 - a
decline from its
height in 1850,
when 899 souls were
recorded spread
through its 4958
acres, 1 rood and 27
perches. In the
background, below
the summit of the
hill, is a sight rarely
seen today -
harvested corn
drying in stooks.

BERRYNARBOR

BERRYNARBOR
The Village c1955 B73042

Hurtisberie, Berry Narbert, Berry-in-Herber, Bury Nerber - the village has had many names, but the constant component of all of them has been Berry, the name of the family who built their manor here in 1480. They had been around for some time before that, however, perhaps as far back as the reign of Athelstan in the 10th century, and they held the manor until 1780.

BERRYNARBOR,
The Post Office and the Church 1934 86453

A directory entry from 1850 mentions George Burgess, who took the post by foot to Ilfracombe each day. Local post, therefore, probably travelled as fast as it does today, but sending mail further afield was a different matter - the mail coach had to travel for several hours to reach the nearest railhead at Tiverton.

▶ **BERRYNARBOR**
*The Village and
the Church 1934*
86450

The 15th-century
church of St Peter is
built from local red
sandstone. Inside, the
arcade is built from
Beer stone - an
expensive item, as
the stone would have
to have been
transported by sea
from East Devon, a
journey of around
300 miles.

◀ **BERRYNARBOR**
The Lees c1960
B73058

Perhaps the village's
most famous son is John
Jewel, born at Bowden
farmhouse in 1522. He
eventually became
Bishop of Salisbury, and
in 1562 wrote *Apologia
pro Ecclesia Anglicana*, a
document considered so
important by Elizabeth I
that she ordered it to be
read in all the churches
of the land.

◄ BERRYNARBOR
Ye Old Globe Inn c1965
B73090

The Globe started life around 1280 as a row of five cottages, possibly built to house masons working on the church. Three of the cottages were converted to become the pub in 1675. The lime-ash floors of the Globe are over 400 years old.

WATERMOUTH
The Harbour 1890
22951

Watermouth's narrow entrance, guarded by the great bulk of Widmouth Head (centre) to the west and Sexton's Burrow opposite, makes it one of the safer, more sheltered harbours on this inhospitable coast; Watermouth is exposed to the full force of the weather only in north-westerly storms.

WATERMOUTH

WATERMOUTH
The Harbour c1871 5895

Trading schooners are
beached, waiting for their
cargo to be taken ashore by
horse and cart. Watermouth
was not always so tranquil,
however - the great tidal surge
of 1910 which so severely
damaged the seafront at
Ilfracombe is recorded to have
thrown ships like these
hundreds of yards inland and
left them high and dry not far
from the castle.

▶ **WATERMOUTH**
*The Castle and
the Bay c1890*
2074B

Despite its almost
Tudor appearance,
Watermouth Castle is
relatively modern,
built in 1825 by
Arthur Bassett for his
bride Harriet. The
castle was a major
employer; besides the
domestic staff of 40
there were flour and
timber mills to run,
oyster beds, and
gardens, which
included hothouses
growing everything
from citrus fruit to
bananas.

◀ **WATERMOUTH**
The Castle c1890
2075B

It is thought there may
have been an ancient
castle here, built to ward
off the attentions of the
pirates who operated in
the Bristol Channel. The
area was also popular
with smugglers, who
used the series of tunnels
which run from the
terrace down to the cove.

▲ **WATERMOUTH,** *The Castle and Hangman Hills c1965* W39153

In World War II the castle was the HQ for Pluto - Pipe Line Under The Ocean - an operation which ran fuel from Liverpool through Wales and across the Bristol Channel and eventually supplied the fleet for the D-Day landings.

◀ **WATERMOUTH**
The Castle, the Hall c1965 W39204

By the 1960s, time had taken its toll on the castle and it was in a poor state of repair. The future looked bleak until the Haines family bought Watermouth in 1977 at the knockdown price of £50,000, and then spent over £1,000,000 on restoration.

WATERMOUTH, *Briery Cave 1898* 43123

Briery Cave is a small example of a feature found all along the Exmoor coast, collapsed caves; these are known locally as
'guts'. One of the most spectacular is North Cleave Gut, 120 yards deep and ten yards wide, with a 350ft waterfall at its head.

INDEX

ILFRACOMBE: THE HARBOUR
Coronation Terrace 20
Entrance to the Harbour 18
Fore Street 27
Harbour 16-17, 21, 22, 24, 25, 26
Hillsborough 22, 23
Pier 19
Pier Entrance 19
Rapparee 20
Rapparee Cove 14-15, 18-19
St James's Gardens 24
Velindra approaching the Pier 20-21

**ILFRACOMBE: LANTERN HILL
AND CAPSTONE HILL**
Beach 41
Capstone Parade 30-31, 40
From Capstone Hill 30-31, 32-33, 37, 38-39
From the Tors 28-29
Hillsborough and Lantern Hill 36-37
Landmark Theatre 34-35
Lantern Hill 28-29, 37
Sunset 36

ILFRACOMBE: THE PROMENADE
Bath House 52
Bathing Pool 52-53
Belgrave Hotel 54-55
Capstone Hill 42-43, 46-47, 50-51
Carlton Hotel 53
Collingwood and the Shelter 42

Feeding the Sea Gulls 51
Ladies' Bathing Beach 52
Parade and the Bandstand 49
Parish Church 55
Parish Church and the Garden of
Remembrance 55
Promenade 44, 48
St Philip's Church 44
Tors Park from the Zigzag 54
Victoria Pavilion 44-45
Victoria Promenade 50

**ILFRACOMBE: THE EDGE
OF THE TOWN**
Cairn from the West 59
Chambercombe Valley 59
From the Torrs 58-59
Slade Valley from the Cairn 58
Torrs Walk 56-57

HELE AND LEE
Bay and Hillsborough 60-61
Coast Road to Lee 62
From the Cliffs 62
From the Golf Links 63
Old Maids Cottage 64
Post Office 63, 64

MORTEHOE
Bull Point Lighthouse 67
Church 68
Morte Point 65

Rockham Beach 67
Windy Point, Morte Point 66

COMBE MARTIN
A Devon Lane 72-73
A Rest on the Way to Hangman Hill 70
Bay 69
Church and the War Memorial 72
General View 71
Harbour 73
Hunter's Inn 70
Newbury Beach 76-77
Pack of Cards Hotel 73
Sandy Cove 76
Seaside Hill and the Harbour 76
Sterrage Valley 77
Strand 74-75
Woodlands and Furze Park 70-71

BERRYNARBOR
Lees 80
Post Office and the Church 79
Village and the Church 80-81
Village 78-79
Village Street 78
Ye Old Globe Inn 81

WATERMOUTH
Briery Cave 86
Harbour 82-83
Watermouth Castle 84-85

NAMES OF SUBSCRIBERS

The following people have kindly supported this book
by subscribing to copies before publication.

Sue Bidgood, Slade Road, Ilfracombe

D. & L. Boreham

Maurice Bryant, Ilfracombe

In Memory of Barry T. Caine

Mr R. N. & Mrs C. M. Catling, Combe Martin

The Chapple Family, Ilfracombe

Jessica Charley

Ernest William Lewis Cook

Fred G. Cooke, Ilfracombe

Eric John Couling

The Cresser Family, Ilfracombe

Jan Cross IMVC

H. Dawson and Family of Ilfracombe

Dee's Marine Court Hotel Memories

The Dickenson Family

Ann Doody, Elmfield Hotel

Miss Betty Dudley-Ward, Berrynarbor

Adam W. Fellows, Ilfracombe

David Fisher, Ilfracombe

The Fox-Newbold Family

Pete & Karen French, Ilfracombe

Ziba Mary German, Coventry

Annie Lez Ghia & Navarre Shiloh Cann

Mrs M. E. Goodridge

Davina M. Hannam

The Hardwick Family, Ilfracombe

Mr P. S. & Mrs N. M. Heard

In Memory of Arthur G. Hibberd, Ilfracombe

Hollie Hopson

In Memory of Kingsley Houlford 1914-2000

John & Veronica Hussell

Michael & Joan James, Doone Way, Ilfracombe

Paul Jennings, Ireland

Sean Jennings, Australia

Betty Karslake, Ilfracombe

John Karslake, Ilfracombe

Mr D. Lane, Ilfracombe, Devon

The Lewis Family, Ilfracombe

Mr G. J. & Mrs D. L. Llewellyn-Rees, Ilfracombe

Olwen & Vic Lusty, Combe Martin

The Meadlarkin Family, Ilfracombe

Mum & Dad Christmas 2004 love Clare

Happy Birthday Mum love Karen & Nigel xx

Karen & Nigel Mytton, Ilfracombe

The Newman Family, Ilfracombe

Bob & Yvonne Newman, Ilfracombe

Mrs C. Oake (nee Heard)

Mr A. C. & Mrs E. M. Parsons, Ilfracombe

Mr A. W. Pennington, Ilfracombe

Miss T. Pennington, Ilfracombe

Iris Perriam

W. J. Phillips Family of Ilfracombe

J. M. Phillips & G. R. Phillips 2004

Robin, Emma & Jack Pickering, Madeley

Mr Robert Pinfield, Studley, Warks

Archie John Porter, Ilfracombe

R. Prideaux

Tony Redmore & Family, Ilfracombe

Margaret & Peter Robins, Ilfracombe

Jeanne Rumson-Waltho and Family

Alison Saunders

Mr S. P. & Mrs G. A. Smith

The Spurway Family, Ilfracombe

Ian & Cynthia Stuart, Lincombe, Lee

Truda Grafton Viney

David George Williams and Family, Ilfracombe

Andrew Williams, Ilfracombe

Mr N. E. Williamson

FREE MOUNTED PRINT

Mounted Print
Overall size 14 x 11 inches

Fill in and cut out this voucher and return
it with your remittance for £2.25 (to cover postage and handling). Offer valid for delivery to UK addresses only.

Choose any photograph included in this book.
Your SEPIA print will be A4 in size. It will be mounted in a cream mount with a burgundy rule line (overall size 14 x 11 inches).

**Order additional Mounted Prints
at HALF PRICE (only £7.49 each*)**
If you would like to order more Frith prints from this book, possibly as gifts for friends and family, you can buy them at half price (with no additional postage and handling costs).

Have your Mounted Prints framed
For an extra £14.95 per print* you can have your mounted print(s) framed in an elegant polished wood and gilt moulding, overall size 16 x 13 inches (no additional postage and handling required).

---

* IMPORTANT!
These special prices are only available if you order at the same time as you order your free mounted print. You must use the ORIGINAL VOUCHER on this page (no copies permitted). We can only despatch to one address.

Send completed Voucher form to:
The Francis Frith Collection, Frith's Barn, Teffont, Salisbury, Wiltshire SP3 5QP

CHOOSE ANY IMAGE FROM THIS BOOK

Voucher for **FREE** and Reduced Price Frith Prints

Please do not photocopy this voucher. Only the original is valid, so please fill it in, cut it out and return it to us with your order.

Picture ref no	Page no	Qty	Mounted @ £7.49	Framed + £14.95	Total Cost
		1	Free of charge*	£	£
			£7.49	£	£
			£7.49	£	£
			£7.49	£	£
			£7.49	£	£
			£7.49	£	£

Please allow 28 days for delivery

* Post & handling (UK)	**£3.50**
Total Order Cost	**£**

Title of this book . . . .

I enclose a cheque/postal order for £ . . . .
made payable to 'The Francis Frith Collection'

OR please debit my Mastercard / Visa / Switch / Amex card
(credit cards please on all overseas orders), details below

Card Number

Issue No (Switch only)   Valid from (Amex/Switch)

Expires   Signature

Name Mr/Mrs/Ms . . . .

Address . . . .

. . . .

. . . .

. . . . Postcode . . . .

Daytime Tel No . . . .

Email . . . .

VALID TO 31/12/08

Free Print – see overleaf

Would you like to find out more about Francis Frith?

We have recently recruited some entertaining speakers who are happy to visit local groups, clubs and societies to give an illustrated talk documenting Frith's travels and photographs. If you are a member of such a group and are interested in hosting a presentation, we would love to hear from you.

Our speakers bring with them a small selection of our local town and county books, together with sample prints. They are happy to take orders. A small proportion of the order value is donated to the group who have hosted the presentation. The talks are therefore an excellent way of fundraising for small groups and societies.

Can you help us with information about any of the Frith photographs in this book?

We are gradually compiling an historical record for each of the photographs in the Frith archive. It is always fascinating to find out the names of the people shown in the pictures, as well as insights into the shops, buildings and other features depicted.

If you recognize anyone in the photographs in this book, or if you have information not already included in the author's caption, do let us know. We would love to hear from you, and will try to publish it in future books or articles.

Our production team

Frith books are produced by a small dedicated team at offices in the converted Grade II listed 18th-century barn at Teffont near Salisbury, illustrated above. Most have worked with the Frith Collection for many years. All have in common one quality: they have a passion for the Frith Collection. The team is constantly expanding, but currently includes:

Paul Baron, Jason Buck, John Buck, Ruth Butler, Heather Crisp, David Davies, Isobel Hall, Julian Hight, Peter Horne, James Kinnear, Karen Kinnear, Tina Leary, Stuart Login, David Marsh, Sue Molloy, Glenda Morgan, Wayne Morgan, Kate Rotondetto, Dean Scource, Eliza Sackett, Terence Sackett, Sandra Sampson, Adrian Sanders, Sandra Sanger, Julia Skinner, Claire Tarrier, Lewis Taylor, Shelley Tolcher, Lorraine Tuck and Jeremy Walker.